THE PRESIDENTS OF
THE UNITED STATES
OF AMERICA

THE PRESIDENTS OF THE UNITED STATES OF AMERICA

text by

Nicholas Best

A Bulfinch Press Book
Little, Brown and Company
Boston • New York • Toronto • London

First North American Edition

First published in 1995 by
[George] Weidenfeld & Nicolson [Limited]
The Orion Publishing Group

ISBN 0-8212-2256-2

Library of Congress Catalog Card Number 95-78071

Bulfinch Press is an imprint and trademark of
Little, Brown and Company (Inc.)

Published simultaneously in Canada by
Little, Brown & Company (Canada) Limited

PRINTED IN ITALY

Contents

GEORGE WASHINGTON
1789–1797

Himself descended from English kings, Washington was the obvious choice to become President of the world's first republic. Born in 1732, he grew up a Virginia landowner and played a major part in the revolt against English rule, eventually forcing the surrender of Lord Cornwallis's army at Yorktown.

Such was his stature and integrity that he was elected President with only token opposition. In common with England's King George III, he regarded himself as above party politics and did his best not to become involved. He was an aloof, cold man, admired rather than loved. He was re-elected in 1792 but declined to run again in 1796, returning instead to Virginia, where he died in 1799. Washington set a standard of leadership which all subsequent Presidents have sought – mostly in vain – to follow.

John Adams

Born in 1735, Adams was a Harvard-trained lawyer who defended the British troops accused of the Boston massacre – an act of considerable courage – but later helped draft the American Declaration of Independence. He served as Vice-President under Washington and was elected in his own right after Washington retired.

Small, round and vain – known as 'His Rotundity' – Adams tried without success to discourage the development of a party political system. He supported the Alien and Sedition Laws of 1798, which curtailed freedom of speech in an attempt to discourage the spread of ideas from the French Revolution. As a result, he was not re-elected in 1800, but retired to Massachusetts instead, dying in 1826. If Washington was the father of the nation, Adams was the father of the US Navy and the first President to live in the building now known as the White House.

Th: Jefferson

THOMAS JEFFERSON
1801–1809

Statesman, scientist, philosopher, inventor, agriculturalist – Jefferson was a major figure in American history and a great man by any standard. A lawyer by training (born in Virginia in 1743), he was the chief author of the Declaration of Independence. All its finest phrases were his.

Jefferson spent eight uncongenial years as President, leading the 'Democratic Republicans' (who favoured the rights of individual states) against the 'Federalists' (who believed in strong national government). In 1803 he doubled the size of the US with the Louisiana Purchase from the French Government and a year later sent Lewis and Clark to explore the new land. He returned to Virginia on leaving the Presidency and died in 1826 after many happy years managing his estates, where – among other things – he grew America's first tomato.

James Madison (signature)

JAMES MADISON
1809–1817

Madison was Secretary of State under Jefferson and succeeded his friend and fellow Virginian as President. Born in 1751, he was a small but very bright lawyer who drafted much of the US constitution, devising a system of government that did its best to balance the differing needs of the individual states and the central executive.

Unfortunately Madison was less able as a military leader. He allowed Napoleon to dupe him into trade sanctions against Great Britain, with the result that the British stormed Washington during the War of 1812 and set fire to Madison's official residence – though not before stealing his hat. The building was repainted to hide the scorch marks and has been the White House ever since. Madison's reputation was retrieved by the battle of New Orleans and he later retired to Virginia, where he died in 1836.

James Monroe

JAMES MONROE
1817–1825

In common with three of his four predecessors, Monroe was from Virginia. Born in 1758, he fought in the revolutionary war and served as a diplomat before becoming President. His election coincided with a spirit of national unity known as the Era of Good Feelings and he was elected virtually unopposed.

Monroe was a dull, formal man, content to consolidate the achievements of his predecessors rather than introduce any great initiatives of his own. But he was responsible for the Monroe Doctrine, asserting that the American continent was not to be colonized by any European power. And he arranged the Missouri Compromise, which allowed Missouri to enter the Union as a slave state – a subject of growing controversy. Monroe himself opposed slavery (Monrovia in Liberia is named after him). He died in reduced circumstances in 1831.

John Quincy Adams

JOHN QUINCY ADAMS
1825–1829

Son of the second President, Adams (born 1767) witnessed the battle of Bunker Hill as a boy and was US ambassador to Russia during Napoleon's invasion of 1812. He was also a Harvard professor, a published poet and a distinguished Secretary of State, responsible for much of the shaping of modern America that took place under President Monroe. Adams' only real failure was the four years he himself spent as President.

Austere and intellectual, he disliked party politics and made no effort to win friends on Capitol Hill. His election was bitterly opposed by supporters of Andrew Jackson, who felt their candidate had been cheated of victory. Jackson did win in 1828, denying Adams (like his father) a second term. Adams then spent 17 years in Congress, distinguishing himself as 'Old Man Eloquent'. He was in Congress when he died of a stroke in 1848.

Andrew Jackson

ANDREW JACKSON
1829–1837

Unlike any of his predecessors, Jackson was a man of the people. The son of Irish immigrants, he was born in 1767 and grew up poor in South Carolina, later moving to Tennessee. From the age of 14 he carried a scar on his cheek from the sword of a British officer whose boots he had refused to clean. Jackson got his revenge in 1815, when he defeated the British at the battle of New Orleans, becoming a national hero in the process.

Deeply distrustful of politicians, Jackson fired hundreds of office holders when he became President, replacing them with his own men. He believed 'rotation in office' would eliminate corruption, but in fact his spoils system tended to reward loyalty above efficiency and he was mocked by insiders for his tobacco-chewing, homespun ways. Yet ordinary people loved him for those qualities. He died in Tennessee in 1845.

MARTIN VAN BUREN
1837–1841

Van Buren was born in 1782, too young to remember the revolutionary war. From a very early age he was a machine politician of a kind Americans hadn't seen before, promising jobs to his friends in return for their support. His first base was the 'Albany Regency' in New York, but he later became Secretary of State under Andrew Jackson and in due course succeeded him as President.

Small, sly and charming, Van Buren carried the art of political manipulation to new heights, earning himself the nickname 'Little Magician' on the way. He never committed himself to any particular policy if there was a chance of sitting on the fence. But he was unseated by the Panic of 1837, when speculators bought land with paper money, causing a run on the banks and a nation-wide depression. Van Buren was not re-elected in 1840 – or in 1844 or 1848. He died in 1862.

WILLIAM HENRY HARRISON
1841

Harrison's father was a signatory to the Declaration of Independence. He himself was the last President to have been born (in 1773) a British subject. He grew up in Virginia but made his name as Governor of Indiana, where he pushed the Indian tribes off their land and won a decisive battle at Tippecanoe.

Known thereafter as Old Tip, he cultivated a log cabin, coonskin cap image, although he had in fact been born into the plantocracy. Having also won one of the few American victories in the War of 1812, he was an obvious candidate to run against Van Buren in 1840. 'Say nothing, promise nothing' advised his managers, and Harrison duly won a landslide victory. But he was 68 at his inauguration and the election campaign had exhausted him. Harrison developed pneumonia and died in April 1841 after only 31 days in office.

John Tyler

JOHN TYLER
1841–1845

It is said that Tyler (born 1790) was on his hands and knees, playing marbles, when news reached him of President Harrison's death. As Vice-President, he immediately took over the job, although nobody was sure if he was President in his own right or merely acting President. He was nicknamed 'His Accidency' and largely ignored by his own Cabinet. All but one resigned after a few months, leaving Tyler to struggle on by himself for the rest of his presidency.

Despite these setbacks, Tyler was the man who brought Texas into the Union and signed the 'Log Cabin' bill, enabling homesteaders to buy 160 acres each of public land. He did not seek a second term as President, retiring instead to Virginia. In 1861 he chaired a conference to avert civil war. When that failed, he joined the Confederacy – the only ex-President to do so – and died in 1862.

JAMES POLK
1845–1849

Dull and straight-laced, Polk was born in North Carolina in 1795. A lawyer by training, he went into state politics, but was always a dark horse for the Presidency. He would never have been elected at all if it hadn't been for the issue of territorial expansion.

In 1844, the US was considering annexing Texas. Since this would provoke Mexico, more prominent candidates than Polk opposed it. But Polk approved of the idea and so did the voters. Emerging from nowhere to win the Presidency, he promptly declared war on Mexico. The US gained Texas as a result, also California (where gold was discovered in 1848) and New Mexico. Polk also secured Oregon for the Union, after negotiating a treaty with the British that left them Vancouver. He rarely left his desk during his time at the White House and died exhausted in 1849, only a few months after leaving office.

ZACHARY TAYLOR

1849–1850

Old 'Rough and Ready' had very little experience of public affairs when he became President. Born in 1784, and with hardly any formal education, he was a soldier, pure and simple. He served in many campaigns, but did not seriously make his name until 1847, when his troops thrashed a vastly superior Mexican army at Buena Vista.

Thereafter Taylor was a shoo-in for the Presidency, though he himself had never bothered to vote in an election – not even for himself. His strength lay in his non-partisan approach at a time of growing national divisions. He had no strong view on the slavery question, which had come to a head with the admission of California and New Mexico to the Union. Should they be slave states or non-slave? Taylor was not well equipped to deal with the ensuing crisis, so it was perhaps fortunate that he died in 1850, after only a year in office.

Millard Fillmore

MILLARD FILLMORE
1850–1853

Like many others, Fillmore was only nominated Vice-President in order to present a balanced ticket to the electorate. So it was a shock when Zachary Taylor died prematurely and Fillmore was dragged blinking into the limelight. He was never really White House material, as even his friends privately acknowledged.

Born in New York in 1800, he was variously an apprentice wool carder, teacher and lawyer before entering politics. Slavery was the issue of the day and _Uncle Tom's Cabin_ was published during his Presidency. Fillmore tried to be all things to all men on the subject, but succeeded only in alienating everyone with a legislative package known as the Compromise of 1850. His party dropped him in 1852 and he retired to a well-deserved obscurity, dying in 1874. But he did install the White House's first ever bath tub.

FRANKLIN PIERCE
1853–1857

A mediocre man, Pierce was one of a series of compromise candidates elected President during the run-up to the Civil War. Born in New Hampshire in 1804 he numbered Hawthorne and Longfellow among his college contemporaries. He trained as a lawyer but also served in the Mexican war – his enemies accused him of fainting on the battlefield, a charge he always denied.

As President he pursued a vigorous foreign policy, planning to seize Cuba from Spain. At home though, he was no more able than anyone else to resolve the slavery dispute. To avoid a confrontation over slavery with the new states of Kansas and Nebraska, he partially revoked the Missouri Compromise of 1820 – thus reopening the whole contentious issue. Pierce was not renominated in 1856, he retired to New Hampshire, where he became an alcoholic and died in 1869.

James Buchanan

James Buchanan
1857–1861

Born in 1791, Buchanan had been a public servant for 40 years before becoming President. He was ambassador to England from 1853–1856 and thus avoided identification with either side in the Kansas slavery crisis – an immeasurable boon during his election campaign.

But his victory was hollow, for he had no chance of reconciling the two sides in an increasingly bitter dispute. As a lawyer, he knew that property owning was guaranteed by the Constitution. Yet the Dred Scott case – when a slave north of the Missouri line was denied his freedom because he was a chattel, not a person – made a mockery of the law. Unable to hold the ring – particularly after John Brown's raid at Harper's Ferry – Buchanan declined to seek re-election. Southern states were already seceding from the Union as he handed over to Abraham Lincoln. He died, still a bachelor, in 1868.

ABRAHAM LINCOLN
1861–1865

One of the greatest Presidents of all, Lincoln was born in a Kentucky log cabin in 1809. From humble origins, he qualified as a lawyer before entering politics. His views on slavery were comparatively moderate, but this did not stop the South from forming a Confederacy under Jefferson Davis rather than remaining in the Union under Lincoln.

The Civil War was fought initially on the right of states to secede from the Union. It was only later that the Union sought to set all slaves free – only as a means of winning the war. Lincoln controlled the war effort himself and delivered at Gettysburg a famous address in favour of democracy. But he had his limitations as a war leader and was not universally admired in his own time. In 1865, five days after the war was won, he was assassinated in a Washington theatre by John Wilkes Booth, a Southern sympathizer.

ANDREW JOHNSON
1865–1869

Born in 1808, apprenticed to a tailor at ten, Johnson never had a day's schooling in his life. By sheer force of character he taught himself to read and write, but remained bitter about his origins to the end of his days.

As senator for Tennessee, Johnson opposed the Confederacy's secession from the Union and was the only Southern senator to support Lincoln in the Civil War. He became Vice-President in 1864 and succeeded Lincoln in 1865, promising retribution against the Southern aristocrats who had grown rich on slavery. In the event though, he pursued a moderate line, sometimes even favouring the whites against the newly freed negroes. This in turn lost him support from northern politicians. Johnson was impeached on a technicality and only escaped by one vote. With no prospect of re-election, he retired thoroughly disillusioned and died in Tennessee in 1875.

U. Grant (signature)

ULYSSES GRANT
1869–1877

The Civil War made Grant. Born in Ohio in 1822, he had been an army officer before the war, but had been forced to resign for drunkenness. He was working as a clerk when the attack on Fort Sumter gave him the chance to re-enlist. A brilliant commander, he ultimately became the first full General since Washington and received General Robert E. Lee's surrender at Appomattox Court House.

Grant's big mistake was to accept the Presidency in 1869. Like so many soldiers, he wasn't cut out for the job. He was a poor judge of politicians and many of his appointments turned out to be corrupt. Everyone was relieved when his second term came to an end. After taking a trip around the world, he lost all his money in a banking collapse and wrote his memoirs to support his family. He completed them four days before dying of cancer of the tongue in 1885.

RUTHERFORD HAYES

1877–1881

Hayes didn't even know if he was President until two days before his inauguration. The vote had been so close, the ballot rigging so blatant, that the issue had to be decided by an electoral commission appointed for the purpose. Even so, Hayes had to pledge the withdrawal of federal troops from the South before the Democrats would allow his inauguration to proceed.

A Harvard lawyer and Civil War general, Hayes was born in Ohio in 1822. His appeal lay in his transparent honesty, a refreshing change from the corruption of the Grant years. He despised the spoils system of the Civil Service and did his best to reform it. As part of his election deal, he also withdrew the last of the Yankee carpetbagger governments from the South, leaving the old Confederate states to their own (white supremacist) devices. He declined a second term, and died in 1893.

JAMES GARFIELD
1881

The third President in a row to be a Civil War general from Ohio, Garfield was born poor in 1831. As a boy, he worked as a labourer on the Ohio canal before putting himself through college and becoming a classics professor. He sat in Congress for many years, but was virtually unknown when the Republicans made him their Presidential candidate on the 36th ballot.

Garfield took office during the Gilded Age, when the winner's supporters expected as of right to receive jobs and favours for themselves and their friends. Garfield's failure to oblige caused immediate offence. Four months into his first term, he was shot in the back by a disappointed job seeker, Charles Guiteau. He lingered for weeks before dying of blood poisoning in September 1881. His death shocked Congress into cleaning up the spoils system with the Civil Service Reform Act of 1883.

CHESTER ARTHUR
1881–1885

Arthur is said to have been born in Vermont in
1830, but may actually have been born in
Canada in 1829 (which would have made him
ineligible to be President). He emerged from the
corrupt world of New York politics to be Vice-
President under Garfield, representing the
Stalwart wing of the Republican party. When
Garfield was assassinated the Stalwarts rejoiced,
assuming that their man in the White House
would immediately reinstate the spoils system
with all the rewards it entailed.

They were wrong. After a hitherto unimpres-
sive career, Arthur blossomed in the White
House. Far from handing out jobs for the boys,
he reformed the system instead, insisting that
appointments 'should be based upon a certain
fitness'. His attitude cost him the approval of the
Stalwarts, who refused to support him in 1884.
He retired gracefully and died two years later.

GROVER CLEVELAND

1885–1889, 1893–1897

The first Democratic President for 28 years, Cleveland was also the only President to serve two non-consecutive terms and the only one to get married at the White House. In an age of widespread corruption, he was a beacon of honesty and integrity in American public life.

Born in New Jersey in 1837, he started out as a lawyer's clerk and soon built up his own practice. Despite staying at home during the Civil War – to look after his mother – he was elected Governor of New York and used that as a springboard for the Presidency. The only scandal in his life was an illegitimate child, openly admitted. Cleveland won the election and proved a good servant to the nation. But his financial stringency cost him his re-election. He spent the next four years as a lawyer before returning to the White House in 1893. He retired for good in 1897, dying at Princeton in 1908.

BENJAMIN HARRISON
1889–1893

As the grandson of a President (William Henry Harrison) and great-grandson of a signatory to the Declaration of Independence, Harrison came from the nearest American equivalent to a Royal family. It was for his lineage, rather than any particular talents of his own, that the Republicans made him their candidate for the Presidency in 1888.

He was born in Ohio, always a key electoral state, in 1833. His circumstances were relatively modest, but he became a lawyer and a Civil War general before representing Indiana in the Senate. As President, he was intelligent and honest, but 'cold as an iceberg' and widely ignored. He allowed the spoils system to flourish again and had little influence over Congress. Harrison was unseated by Cleveland in 1892 and returned to Indianapolis, where he died in 1901.

WILLIAM MCKINLEY
1897–1901

Born in Ohio in 1843, McKinley served in the Civil War and was Governor of his home state before entering the White House. He was a highly experienced politician and made an excellent job of running the country. The US became a world power under his Presidency, fighting a war with Spain – which led to the independence of Cuba and the annexation of Puerto Rico, Guam and the Philippines – taking over Hawaii and joining other leading nations in policing China during the Boxer rebellion.

McKinley himself had doubts about colonial expansionism, but was carried along by his compatriots. His private life was troubled – his daughters died in childhood and his wife was an invalid – but he was hugely popular with the voters. He won a resounding second victory in 1900, only to be assassinated the following year by a self-styled anarchist in Buffalo, New York.

Theodore Roosevelt

THEODORE ROOSEVELT
1901–1909

Few Presidents captured the public imagination as completely as Roosevelt. Rancher, hunter, Rough Rider, vigilante, patriot, imperialist, Nobel laureate and champion of the working man, he was the person millions of Americans would have liked to be, if only they could.

Dutch in origin, he was born into a family of New York bankers in 1858. He compensated for a sickly childhood by boxing at Harvard and hunting bears in the woods. After a spell ranching in North Dakota, he became Assistant Navy Secretary under McKinley, but gave it up to join the Rough Riders in the Spanish war, where he distinguished himself at the battle of San Juan. He became Vice-President in 1901, succeeding McKinley the same year. As President, he protected the national parks for the nation, secured the Panama Canal, and curbed the worst excesses of big business. He died in 1919.

WILLIAM TAFT
1909–1913

An able lawyer (born in Ohio, 1857), Taft never wanted to be President. He wanted to be Chief Justice. But his wife was much more ambitious – she arranged with his friend Roosevelt to secure the Republican nomination for him after Roosevelt retired.

Himself the son of an Attorney General, Taft served as Solicitor General and Governor of the Philippines before becoming President – with Roosevelt's backing. But Taft was lethargic in office where Roosevelt was energetic, cautious and legalistic where Roosevelt would shoot from the hip. So exasperated did Roosevelt become with his protégé's unwillingness to lead from the front that he came out of retirement to run against him in the election of 1912. His intervention split the vote and both lost. Taft retired happily and became Chief Justice of the US – just what he had always wanted! He died in 1930.

WOODROW WILSON
1913–1921

An academic lawyer and constitutional scholar, Wilson went from President of Princeton University to President of the USA in only two years. It was an extraordinary rise, but then Wilson was an extraordinary man.

He was born in Virginia in 1856, the son of a Presbyterian minister, and was a professor of jurisprudence before becoming Governor of New Jersey and Democratic candidate for President. His Presidency was dominated by the First World War, which began in 1914. Wilson did his best to keep the US neutral and succeeded until German attacks on US shipping proved too much. An outstanding war leader, he also represented America at the peace conference which followed, but couldn't persuade the Senate to ratify the Treaty of Versailles or endorse the League of Nations. Paralysed by a stroke in 1919, he retired in 1921 and died three years later.

WARREN HARDING
1921–1923

Harding was probably the most inept and certainly the most corrupt President of all. He had, as Woodrow Wilson contemptuously put it, a 'bungalow mind' and was gravely out of his depth as President of his country.

Born in Ohio in 1865, he was a small town newspaper editor and convivial poker player before becoming a US senator. His nomination for the Presidency was organized by Republican party managers and good old boys in smoke-filled rooms. As President, Harding adopted the slogan "less government in business, more business in government", but he also gave jobs to his poker-playing buddies who creamed off millions from the public purse in return. Harding himself was too busy hiding his mistress from his wife in White House closets to do anything about it. But the scandals did not surface until later, so he was widely mourned when he died of a stroke in 1923.

CALVIN COOLIDGE
1923–1929

Untainted by the corruption of the Harding years, Vice-President Coolidge moved smoothly into the White House on his predecessor's death and immediately set about restoring the prestige of the Presidency. He believed that 'the business of America is business' and that his job as President was to sit back and do nothing, rather than interfere unnecessarily.

He was born in Vermont in 1872, but made his career as a lawyer in Massachusetts before becoming Governor. Part-Indian, puritanical of mind, he was an unlikely President in the Jazz Age, but his *laisser-faire* policies benefited American business enormously, not least Henry Ford's. He knew little about foreign policy and opposed the League of Nations, but was hugely popular in smalltown America. It was a blow to the country when he refused to run for a second full term. He died in 1933.

HERBERT HOOVER

1929–1933

Hoover's misfortune was to be elected President just as a great wave of prosperity came to an end. The Wall Street crash of 1929 and the Great Depression of the early 1930s left more than 12 million people out of work. Hoover's Presidency never recovered.

Born poor in Iowa in 1874, he started out as a gold miner, working in Australia and China, but soon became a millionaire. As a self-made man, he was a popular choice to succeed Coolidge as President. But he was a prisoner of his conviction that there was little the Government either could or should do to halt the deepening Depression. The homeless all over America named their shanty towns 'Hoovervilles' in protest. Hoover was overwhelmingly rejected by the voters in 1932 and retired to California. His reputation recovered in later years and he died, a grand old man, in 1964.

FRANKLIN ROOSEVELT
1933–1945

The second member of the family to become President, Roosevelt saw America through the Great Depression and led his country to victory in the Second World War. He was a giant on the world stage and one of the greatest men of the century.

Born rich in 1882, he was crippled by polio at 39 but never wavered in his Presidential ambitions. He trounced Hoover in 1932, promising a New Deal for America, and spent his first hundred days in office introducing all sorts of Government measures to create jobs. The economy slowly recovered, then boomed in the Second World War. Roosevelt played a crucial part both in winning the war and in shaping the peace that followed. But an unprecedented four terms in office took its toll. He died exhausted in April 1945 – a few weeks short of the war's end. All of the free world mourned.

Harry Truman
1945–1953

From humble beginnings as a failed Missouri haberdasher (he repaid all his creditors), Vice-President Truman stepped into Roosevelt's shoes in 1945 to become the most powerful man in the world, the first in history to have an atom bomb at his disposal.

Born in 1884, he worked at a variety of dull jobs before turning to politics. His appeal lay in his apparent ordinariness, but he was no fool. He took the decision to drop two atom bombs on Japan, but also helped establish the United Nations, NATO and the Marshall Plan for reconstructing Europe. The Truman doctrine of 1947 abandoned America's long isolationist stance and pledged the US to support free nations against armed aggression, an ideal which led to the Cold War against Communism, and to the Korean and Vietnam wars. Truman retired in 1953, dying in Kansas City, Missouri, 19 years later.

DWIGHT EISENHOWER

1953–1961

As Supreme Commander of the Allied forces that beat Hitler, Eisenhower was an American war hero, even though he had never been in a battle. He refused a Presidential nomination in 1948, but won by a landslide in 1952.

He was born in Texas in 1890, and grew up in Kansas, the son of a mechanic. A career soldier before the White House, he believed in delegating authority, sometimes more than was prudent. Senator McCarthy flourished under his Presidency, blacklisting Communists for their political beliefs. But Eisenhower promoted civil rights for Afro-Americans, sending troops to Little Rock, Arkansas in 1957 to enforce the desegregation of schools. He was a simple, decent man, much liked even by his opponents. In 1961 he retired to his farm at Gettysburg, after warning of the dangers of the 'military-industrial complex'. He died in 1969.

JOHN KENNEDY
1961–1963

No modern Presidency was more glamorous – or more tragic – than Kennedy's. After the torpor of the Eisenhower years, he galvanized his country in a way no other recent President has ever done.

He was born in 1917, to a family of self-made Irishmen. After a gilded youth, including a spell as a war hero, he won a tight race to become the first Roman Catholic in the White House. In a TV age, he was greatly helped by his youth and charm, and by his wife's glamour. The Kennedys brought enormous elegance to Washington, talking boldly of a New Frontier for their country and the world. Privately though, their marriage was not perfect and Kennedy's decision-making was often flawed. He was assassinated in Dallas in 1963, perhaps as the result of a conspiracy. Millions all over the world still remember what they were doing when they heard the news.

Lyndon B. Johnson
1963-1969

Vice-President Johnson was sworn in as President on a plane about to fly back to Washington from Dallas. Next to him stood President Kennedy's widow, her dress still covered in her husband's blood.

Born in Texas in 1908, Johnson did his best to continue Kennedy's liberal policies, but in a country more divided than at any time since the Civil War. At home, Afro-Americans were rioting in the ghettoes for civil rights. Abroad, the Vietnam war was increasingly unpopular, leading to violent campus demonstrations across America. Robert Kennedy and Martin Luther King were both gunned down, causing despair to millions. Boorish and earthy, he liked to give interviews on the lavatory, Johnson was not the man to heal the nation's wounds. He bowed out in 1969 and died in 1973 – a day before the Vietnam war finally ended.

RICHARD NIXON
1969–1974

Nixon has gone down in history as the only President ever to resign – forced to do so, to avoid being impeached for his part in the Watergate scandal. Yet in many ways he was one of America's most dedicated and effective Presidents.

From modest beginnings (born a Quaker in 1913), he was a machine politician for most of his life before becoming President. A highly sophisticated man, he held his own with foreign leaders in a way few Presidents have ever done. He made it his business to end the Vietnam War, and defused the Cold War by recognizing China and negotiating a limitation of nuclear arms. Yet all Nixon is ever remembered for is his attempt to cover up the Watergate burglary, when his supporters raided Democratic headquarters during his re-election campaign. He resigned, disgraced, in 1974.

GERALD FORD

1974–1977

Vice-President Agnew had earlier resigned on tax evasion charges, so there was no one to succeed Nixon when he himself resigned in 1974. Into this breach stepped Congressman Ford, the only President never to be elected by the nation.

His real name was King. Born in Nebraska in 1913, he took his stepfather's name and moved to Michigan, from where he entered Congress as a Republican. Decent, dull, diligent, untainted by scandal, he was nominated by Nixon to succeed Agnew as Vice-President and in due course succeeded Nixon himself. He immediately granted his predecessor a pardon for Watergate – a controversial decision at the time, but one which helped to heal an unhappy episode in the nation's history. Yet Ford's was always a lame duck Presidency, so it was inevitable that the voters would insist on a complete change in 1977.

Jimmy Carter (signature)

Jimmy Carter

1977–1981

As a Southerner – he was Governor of Georgia – Carter was an outsider, as far removed from Washington politics as it was possible to be. He was a plain, honest, God-fearing man, and in the first election after Watergate the voters turned to him in droves to bring about a new beginning for their country.

Unfortunately, Carter did not adapt well to the larger stage. Born in Plains, Georgia in 1924, he had lived in the same small town all his life, working mostly as a peanut farmer. He brought small town ideas to Washington with him, as well as a team of advisers who did not impress. Carter's main triumph was to negotiate peace between Egypt and Israel. But the world oil shortage, and the Iranian hostage crisis, when US diplomats were taken prisoner, lost him popularity. He was voted out in 1980 and went home to Georgia.

RONALD REAGAN
1981–1989

After a career as sports reporter and Hollywood star, Reagan became, at 69, the oldest man ever to be elected President. He suffered from Alzheimer's disease during his second term and aides had to hold up prompt cards at meetings to remind him what to say.

He was born in Illinois in 1911, but later became Governor of California. Although very right wing, he was an easy going man who took a relaxed attitude to life and liked to watch Westerns in the afternoon. Liberals derided his 'Star Wars' programme, a massive build-up of arms against the Soviet Union. Yet the cost was so great that the Communist system couldn't match it and collapsed. Reagan was a great communicator, skilled at TV presentation. Mistakes by his administration were never attributed to him personally. He retired, much liked, in 1989.

GEORGE BUSH
1989–1993

Widely ignored during eight years as Reagan's Vice-President, Bush came from behind in the polls to succeed Reagan at the White House. He acquitted himself tolerably well, but was never really at ease in the top job.

Educated at prep school and Yale, Bush lacked the common touch as President. He was born in Massachusetts in 1924 and flew against the Japanese in the Pacific before making his fortune as a Texas oilman. He was also ambassador to China and head of the CIA. As President, he played a large role in the Iraqi war, when allied nations sent troops to Kuwait to defeat Sadam Hussein's invasion. Yet Bush somehow never managed to capitalize on the victory. He ran for re-election in 1992, in the middle of a severe economic recession, but was defeated by Bill Clinton, the hitherto unknown governor of Arkansas in 1993.

William Clinton

BILL CLINTON
1993–

As his first term as President draws to a close, Clinton has become the latest in a long line of Chief Executives to discover that the job is actually much harder than it looks from the outside.

Born in 1946, he emerged from modest origins to a Rhodes scholarship at Oxford. There he was alienated by the arrogance of the English upper classes, just as some of the earliest Presidents were on their European tours. After Yale law school, he was Governor of Arkansas before unseating Bush. Clinton promised 100 days of furious activity when he took office, including a health care package for the poor to bring America into line with other industrial nations. But his good intentions were thwarted and he was never able to get the package past Congress – despite the support of his wife Hillary, who had devoted her considerable talent to the project.